D0709484

My First Hundred Years

University of Houston
Music Library
.06 Fine Arts
Houston Texas 77004

Robert Mayer

MY FIRST HUNDRED YEARS

by

SIR ROBERT MAYER

CENTENARY EDITION

VAN DUREN

GERRARDS CROSS 1979

MY FIRST HUNDRED YEARS — Centenary Edition — first published on 5th June 1979 by Van Duren Publishers, Gerrards Cross, Buckinghamshire, England.

ISBN 0-905715-09-8

MY FIRST HUNDRED YEARS Copyright © Sir Robert Mayer, 1971, 1972, 1976, 1979. Previously published in limited editions.

THE ANATOMY OF A MIRACLE Copyright © Sir Robert Mayer, 1972.

REFLECTIONS AND PROJECTIONS ON MUSIC AND YOUTH by Sir Robert Mayer. Reprinted from *Looking Forward to the Seventies* — a Blueprint of British Education; Editor: Peter Bander; © 1968 Colin Smythe Ltd.

The drawing on the book jacket is by Sir Hugh Casson, PRA, who designed it for the centenary celebrations.

The photograph on the frontispiece is by Bern Schwartz.

All other photographs are Copyright © *Youth & Music Ltd.*

The centenary edition of MY FIRST HUNDRED YEARS by Sir Robert Mayer, C.H., is sold in aid of YOUTH & MUSIC, a movement founded by Sir Robert in 1954.

CIP Data:
Mayer, *Sir* Robert, b. 1879
    My first hundred years.
    1. Mayer, *Sir* Robert, b. 1879
    2. Impresarios - Biography
    I. Title   II. Mayer, *Sir* Robert, b. 1879
                        Anatomy of a miracle.
    785'.073   ML 429. M 35
    ISBN 0-905715-09-8

Printed and bound by A. Wheaton & Co. Ltd., Exeter, Devon.

CONTENTS

To my Dorothy

MY FIRST HUNDRED YEARS

Based on an informal address given at the British Institute
of Recorded Sound on 3rd December 1971, revised and
added to by the author on the occasion of his one hundredth
birthday.

MY friends present here tonight know that I am exaggerating in choosing the title for my lecture and that I have taken advantage of literary licence, though my remarks do not pretend to be more than a prosaic recital of events and experiences which have shaped my life. You will have to wait for 1979 before I can truthfully look back on one hundred years existence on this planet.

I WAS born in 1879 in Mannheim, then a quiet, modest little town of 45,000 inhabitants. My father's forbears were hop merchants. Evidently he was ambitious, for he grew a beard to hide his youthfulness, and, according to what he told his three children with pride, he was the first to persuade the Guinesses to buy German hops. He was nicknamed *der schöne Emil;* so it was thanks to his looks, and not his birth, that my maternal grandmother consented to his marrying her daughter, thereby stepping into the Seligman family, which was considered socially superior to his own. In fact, the Seligman Saga is to my mind so exciting that it is worth recounting.

MY great grandmother was the head of a family of twelve who lived in a small Bavarian village. She managed to save sufficient money to send her eldest son to Göttingen University and soon thereafter to the U.S.A. which 150 years ago was considered the land of golden opportunity for German Jews. Of course he travelled steerage; and like the Guggenheims and others, followed the lure of the West where he started his commercial career as a peddlar. It did not take him long to save $500, which enabled his brother to join him and set in motion the gradual immigration of the rest of the brothers and sisters and the rise of the Seligman clan. They moved East and became merchants who kept up contact with Europe. This stood them in particularly good stead at the outbreak of the American Civil War, when they must have imported material from Europe on such a scale as to bring them into close contact with the Government. For at the termination of the war in 1865 President Andrew Johnson invited James, the eldest of the Seligman brothers, to join his Cabinet as Secretary of the Treasury. It seems incredible, but it is true that this poor immigrant was given the chance, after only thirty years working in the States, to become one of its leaders. But he declined; for the nine brothers had agreed that they would always stick together and share in equal parts the profit made in the business. However great the honour which the President wished to confer on him and his clan, the word James had given was sacred. It is difficult to imagine a similar action to-day when expediency overrules principles. This was the pinnacle of the rise of the Seligmans, who became America's leading bankers. But not for long. One of the agreements among the nine brothers, who operated from New York, London, Paris, Frankfort and Vienna, was that the eldest son should take his father's place in the business. My forbears were obviously traditionalists, but the principle was unsound, for the eldest son was not necessarily the best man for the job. However, the other sons were free to follow their own calling and indeed became—in England—painters, lawyers and even fencing champions. Whether the rule of succession caused the disintegration, whether it was partly due to marriage out of the faith, or whether they simply followed the same fate as other dynasties, the fact is that I can think of only one Seligman who is prominent in banking today.

I AM dwelling on this story because my earliest recollection goes back to the frequent visits which my mother paid to her own mother in Frankfort, taking me along. It was always a red letter day for me, as my grandmother lived in considerable luxury and in a city renowned in those days for its elegance and its international flavour. Only in one respect was Mannheim superior: in music, a field which I entered at the age of five years when I played twenty-one little pieces on the piano—with one finger! on the birthday of my mother who then started to teach me. But she was probably the wrong teacher, being emotionally too involved. Anyhow, my family was glad when I was accepted by the Mannheim Conservatoire. I became the pupil of a musician who, apart from being a pianist, was also the influential music critic of the local paper, in which capacity he joined battle for Brahms and against Wagner. This was the burning issue of the time in musical Europe and especially in Mannheim. When I was eight years old I made my one and only public appearance: I played the Beethoven Sonata No. V (Spring Sonata) for violin and piano, winning considerable applause, partly for my playing and partly for the fact that I was too small to reach the pedals, which impressed even the critics. Led by my mother and aunts, my "fans" announced to the world the advent of another Mozart. This was followed by an announcement from my father who, for once ignoring all gallantry, decided against my becoming a professional. He said that even if I were exceptionally talented, the life of a professional musician was bound to be hard unless I could reach the very top of the profession, whereas I could find great enjoyment in music as a gifted amateur. I was much too young to argue with my father; besides, in those days one revered and obeyed one's parents. Hence, I accepted his decision; and his foresight was amply borne out by subsequent developments. Three years later Brahms visited my native city and was honoured by a concert organised by the Conservatoire, the soloists including a pianist. My hopes of being chosen for that role were dashed when I found myself only the runner-up. Nevertheless, I was presented to the great man; and I remember even to-day that he spoke to me and patted me on the back. But I was bitterly disappointed that I did not actually play before him. To console me, my teacher invited me to come with him to the next performance of the *Meistersinger*. Oddly enough during the performance he refused to sit down, on the theory that he could only give his undivided attention to his task by standing, even if the discomfort did last five hours. I did not object; there must have been in me already at that time the seeds of puritanism which developed so strongly as I grew up.

I T was not only my teacher who gave me chances in the world of music. My parents too encouraged their children. As good middle-class citizens they were regular subscribers to operas and plays, which were given in the charming Baroque theatre, the adjoining hall being reserved for concerts. Every Sunday afternoon my two brothers and I made for the opera house, where we invariably occupied the same seats in the gallery to listen to the weekly fare, consisting of Meyerbeer, Lortzing, d'Albert and so forth, with occasional early Wagner. Waiting in the queue for an hour or more was no great hardship, partly owing to my upbringing; for my father was an open-air devotee. For instance, in May he started his "May-cure", and he would take me for a walk every morning at 6 o'clock, just in time to get me to school an hour later. You can imagine my pride when I was included at the ripe age of eight in a walking tour from Basle to Baden-Baden, equipped with a rucksack, and sleeping on straw instead of a bed. This was one of the many things I wanted to do later with my own sons, just as I had dreams of taking them on the Grand Tour. Hitler squashed both ideas.

BUT I am moving rather fast. I think I should go back and emphasise the importance of music in the life of Mannheim. It was the subject of discussion wherever people assembled, whether in the shop owned by the music publisher, a fervent follower of Wagner, or the cigar store where my father and other *cognoscenti* discussed daily and passionately one topic: the previous evening's opera or concert. I am not, of course the only individual who was brought up in this tradition and took it with him to another country. Another was Otto H. Kahn, the great banker, who became the leader and driving force of the Metropolitan Opera in New York.

A PART from music, my parents were obviously concerned with their children's general education. My eldest brother was a special case as he was bed-ridden for three years. My other brother and I, after attending preparatory school, were sent to the *Gymnasium,* the high school which was open to all. My closest friends were the son of an artistic director of the theatre and the son of the local postman. Given my mother's background, not to mention that of my father, who had become a brewer, we were a strange social mixture, though none of us suffered any disadvantage as a result.

F OR my parents there was no uncertainty about the way they dealt with their children. The two eldest went to university to study law and medicine; I was evidently considered cut out for another career, for I left school at fifteen and went into business. I became an apprentice in a firm of lace manufacturers, starting my commercial career at the bottom of the ladder, cleaning ink pots, fetching sausages and beer for my superiors and attending to such other duties as could be entrusted to a greenhorn of fifteen! Although it was a wealthy international firm, clearly the owners did not disdain economy; for my commercial baptism consisted also in retrieving for further use old envelopes and the string used for tying up packages which had been received. At Christmas I received a gold coin which I treasured with great pride—my first earnings. Except for a break of an hour and a half for the mid-day meal, we worked daily over ten hours and three hours on Sunday. The evenings were largely devoted to practising the piano or to lessons in book-keeping and French. As a result of this experience in my youth, I have never been afraid of working seven days a week.

M Y father, like many South Germans, had a hatred of Prussianism; moreover, he paid yearly visits to Ireland and England and had become a passionate Anglophile. It was not surprising, therefore, that he and the family decided when the time came that I was to live in England. As apart from French I had learned only Latin and Greek at school, I also took lessons in English. These took place at

6.30 in the morning so as to allow me to open the office before 8 o'clock. Before I reached the age of seventeen I found myself giving up my German nationality, in order to emigrate to England. In the summer of 1896 I arrived in London literally with merely a case containing pyjamas and a toothbrush. An uncle, an eccentric man of the world, took me in hand and decided that the young German provincial was to be anglicised from the beginning, including sartorially. He had arranged with Isaac Seligman, my grandmother's brother, that I should stay in the latter's house at the beginning. My stay lasted a whole year, thanks to the kindness of Isaac's wife, a remarkable person who—apart from my wife—influenced my life more than any other woman. She came from the distinguished Messel family of Darmstadt which had, incidentally, produced the leading architect in Germany and the doyen of chemists in England. Her children resented the intrusion of a young foreigner into their family life, but she stood by me. She provided an anchor to which I added another when I became a Tolstoyan to the extent that among other habits I gave up smoking which I have never resumed since.

IN business I was first placed with a relative, a London stockbroker, but the job was not demanding enough, I soon switched to the metal business, where I started with a salary of £100 a year. My family in Germany considered that I could not exist on it and proposed to double it. I refused and somehow managed to live on what I earned. I learned to economise; for instance, I shared my bedroom—though not the piano in it—with a Russian friend and business colleague. He was a fantastic fellow, an eccentric and exhibitionist who liked to entertain the people who frequented the then fashionable church parade in Regent's Park with his bicycle trick riding. His father, who lived in Moscow and was a well-known patron of music, had his own quartet, and I dreamed of the day when I would have my own. This was one of the many dreams which were never realised, though in due course, thanks to my wife, I did become a good amateur pianist and a devotee of chamber music.

I WAS ambitious and worked hard in the metal business. As I spoke three languages I was soon sent abroad, often to international conferences, where I discovered that the English have a far better way of handling men and situations than their continental brothers, who are generally too doctrinaire. It is reasonable to assume that no vast change has occurred since; and this thought encourages the hope that when we join the Common Market, we can and will play a leading part. It would be refreshing to see a change in the habit of self-denigration which is the opposite of the feeling that prevailed when I came to this country. Society was stable and confident, even though George Bernard Shaw preached rebelion, trying to convert the middle class to socialism, the fiery Lloyd George had his knife in the aristocracy for using land merely for hunting and shooting, and advocated land reform. It was part of my education to attend the meetings where such men spoke, in addition to filling my evenings with piano practice, French lessons, and laboratory work at King's College where I endeavoured to acquire the rudiments of metallurgy. This was a waste of effort. I soon realised that I was completely unmechanical and unscientific and that I had better concentrate on the things which I could hope to do. It was the beginning of my realization that my job was to buy and sell metals to best possible advantage.

MY non-business life broadened with the arrival in London of my brother, who had a flair for journalism and the theatre which brought him in contact with opera. Thanks to him I met Hans Richter, the great conductor, Emmy Destinn, who was the best ever Aida and Butterfly, and a host of other eminent musicians. I shared in the glamour of his life, which culminated in the coup of bringing to London 'The Merry Widow'. He became the central figure in providing England with continental operettas and plays. Unfortunately he was killed in a tram accident in Vienna in 1927 which ended my connection with operettas and I pursued my first love, chamber music. I regularly attended the Proms at St. James Hall where I worshipped at the shrine of Joachim and other giants.

THE First World War brought enormous changes into everybody's life, including my own. Owing to my German birth—though I had given up my German nationality twenty years before—I did not join the army until 1917. But I was very active in procuring metals and minerals essential for munitions. My firm was indeed so successful that our competitors combined against us. Trading on the ignorance of M.P.'s, they managed to get through Parliament legislation which in effect disenfranchised us. At the end of the war I was therefore without a job. This did not greatly worry me, however. Before the war, I had met a young soprano, Dorothy Moulton. She joined me in music-making for the army and for hospitals, and when I left the army in 1919 we got married.

IN the meantime I had accepted an offer to join a leading American firm of metal producers. In December 1919 we sailed for the States to start a new life. We arrived with prohibition, and our first experience in the New World was the difficulty of procuring a drink for our first Christmas together. We felt rather lost at first, but soon the friendliness of the Americans put an end to that feeling, and the discovery of many of the branches of the still important Seligman family even provided us with relatives. It did not take us long to discover Carnegie Hall, but we were amazed at the very low standard of the music we heard there. Of course in England too, by the end of the war musical life had deteriorated, but the orchestras we heard in New York appalled us. Also, the halls were so overheated that we sank into a sort of coma by the middle of every concert. There was only one symphony orchestra playing regularly, one good quartet—which was on the point of disbanding—and a limited season at the Metropolitan Opera. The concerts which did impress us favourably were those given by Dr. Walter Damrosch on Saturday mornings for an audience of children. We had never heard anything like them before. The conductor, a man of great charm, spoke to the young people about the music he was going to play, gave them a fanciful interpretation of it, and then played them a programme of classical music, making no concession except to make the concert shorter than if the audience had been adult. I little knew then what this experience would mean to me.

I HAD started taking piano lessons with Harold Bauer, and since we had moved to the country there were no neighbours to object to my nightly practising. My elder son was born in May 1920, and by the autumn my wife was able to give her first recital in New York with a programme of Schubert and Schumann *Lieder* which she had given in London in 1918. The war psychosis had been so far forgotten that only a few of the audience left when they heard the songs in their original language.

OUR life thus seemed fixed in its course when my firm decided that it wished to be represented in Europe, and that I should be its representative. In March 1921 I left for home. My wife and son followed me, accompanied by our faithful maid, a typical Londoner, When one of the New York friends who saw them off remarked jokingly that by this move my son might miss the chance of becoming the President of the United States, she haughtily replied that he might go one better by becoming an English gentleman. We bought a house in Regent's Park, and soon filled it with music. We had met many English musicians before we left for America and now they welcomed us back: Arnold Bax, Harriet Cohen, Albert Sammons, Adrian Boult, John Barbirolli and Lionel Tertis were some of them. Then there were others from Europe; our visitor's book shows as its first entry Bela Bartok, followed by Schnabel, Busch, Furtwängler, Bruno Walter, Milhaud and many others. They came largely as the result of my wife's appearances on the continent, which started with a visit in the autumn of 1921 for recitals to Vienna, where she met Egon Wellesz and members of the Schönberg group. To them she brought something till then unknown on the continent: English music, both the old and the very newest. She invited Egon Wellesz to London, where he met at our house the distinguished musical scholar Edward J. Dent, whom he interested in the project to start an International Society for Contemporary Music. Dent agreed to become its

President, and the S.C.M. was practically born in our house. It held its first festival in 1922 in Salzburg when my wife sang songs by Bliss, Bax and other young English composers of the time. On that occasion we met for the first time Hindemith, Szigeti, Elizabeth Schumann and a host of other musicians who were to become leaders in the international field.

IN the same year, on a country walk as I remember, my wife and I happened to be discussing the state of music in Britain, which was still suffering from the effects of the war and the extreme nationalist attitude towards music. As those of us who lived through the First World War can recall, it was then impossible to hear the works of the great German Masters of the 19th century; and even artists like Richard Strauss and Kreisler had to wait three years after the end of the war before they could perform in England. This made the picture very gloomy; even worse was the fear that the radio and the gramophone, then beginning to emerge, would kill concert life as we knew it. The experts were completely wrong; they failed to foresee that in fact these innovations would immeasurably contribute to the nation's musical awakening. We only saw the sad state of affairs and the uninspiring dull way in which music was being taught in school and at home. We wondered what individuals like ourselves could do to help. Suddenly my wife remembered how impressed we had been by Dr. Damrosch's concerts in New York; could I afford to finance something similar? My reply, the one word 'yes', was to revolutionise my life completely. We decided there and then to launch a series of three concerts, blissfully unaware of the tremendous difficulties of doing so in a city like London.

OUR first thought was to form a committee, and we invited to a preliminary meeting George Bernard Shaw, Arnold Bennett, Hugh Walpole and other public figures interested in music, emphasising that the financial responsibility was to be ours. Only Bennett turned up. It taught us early on to rely on ourselves and may account in part for my scarcely enthusiastic attitude to committees.

CENTRAL HALL, WESTMINSTER

ORCHESTRAL CONCERTS
FOR CHILDREN

|||||||||||||||||||||||||||||||||||||||||||||||||||||||||||||||||

Inaugural Concert

Saturday Morning, March 29th,

At **ELEVEN** o'clock.

Programme

Mozart—" Serenade " .. .. Illustrating Stringed Instruments

Wagner—Introduction to Act III of the " Mastersingers " .. Illustrating Strings and Brass combined

Beethoven—" Rondino in E♭" .. .. Illustrating Wood Wind

Tschaikowsky—" 3rd Movement of Symphony No. 4 " Illustrating Strings, Wood Wind & Brass alternating

Beethoven—" Overture Leonore No. 3 " Illustrating combined Strings, Wood Wind, Brass and Drums

Conductor - ADRIAN BOULT

(Who will introduce each item with a few explanatory remarks on the instruments and their uses).

Tickets (Tax free) - 1/- each; a few Reserved at 2/-

May be obtained at the **BOX OFFICE, CENTRAL HALL,** or of
Mme. LILY HENKEL, 72 HAMILTON TERRACE, N.W.8.
(All applications by post must enclose stamped and addressed envelope).

NO ADULT ADMITTED EXCEPT IN CHARGE OF CHILDREN.

The aim of these Concerts is recognized and approved by the following well-known educationalists :

Sir HUGH ALLEN	Sir CYRIL COBB, K.B.E.	Mr. GEOFFREY SHAW
Miss HENRIETTA ADLER, L.C.C.	Dr. SCOTT LIDGETT, L.C.C.	Dr. ARTHUR SOMERVELL
Dr. JOHN E. BORLAND	Sir A. C. MACKENZIE	Miss KATE WALLAS, L.C.C.
Sir FREDERICK BRIDGE		

GRAMOPHONE RECORDS of the Works to be performed are obtainable.

MINIATURE SCORES and PIANO VERSIONS of the Works to be performed are obtainable of Messrs. J. & W. Chester, Ltd., 11 Great Marlborough Street, W.1.

Teachers applying for not less than 10 tickets will receive gratis a programme with analytical notes by Dr. Boult.

CHRISTIAN THE PRINTER, EASTBOURNE

Programme of the first Robert Mayer Concert, March 29th 1923. The conductor was Adrian Boult.

19

Central Hall, Westminster

Orchestral Concerts
✿ ✿ FOR CHILDREN ✿ ✿

Second Concert

Conductor = **Walter H. Damrosch**

Saturday Morning
May 17th, at 11

Programme and
Notes on the Instruments

The second Orchestral Concert was conducted by Walter H. Damrosch on May 17th 1923. Mr. Damrosch's concerts for young people in the United States of America had inspired Dorothy and Robert Mayer to start similar concerts in the United Kingdom.

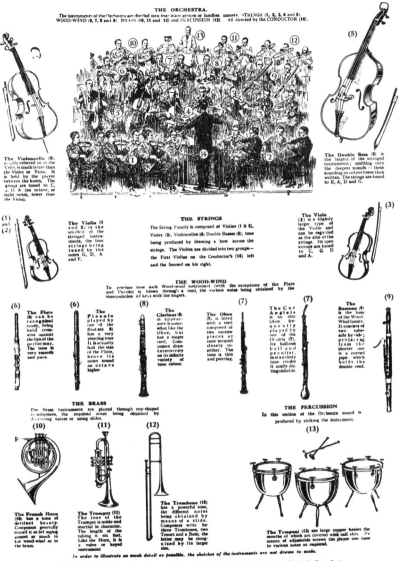

The young audience was introduced to the orchestra and illustrated explanations were given to the children in the programme.

THERE was no law to prevent two pioneers from hiring a hall and an orchestra—which we had to make up specially, as the BBC had the only permanent orchestral body—and a conductor, whom we found in a young friend of ours, Adrian Boult. Public relations consultants did not exist then, but with the help of a telephone directory we mailed thousands of circulars announcing the first concert. The profession was not interested in the scheme, which was generally dismissed as absurd. However, we had a circle of friends with children, and in spite of a strike, a few hundred turned up at the Central Hall for the opening concert, in November 1923. In those far-off days the Press was glad to report on events even though they were not sensational; and at the end of the first series the venture was described as a New Charter in music. Fortunately the notices attracted the attention of the Music Adviser of the London County Council (who incidentally was earning the princely sum of £150 a year); and it was really due to him that we decided to link our operations with the national education system, instead of relying on conventional publicity.

IT would take too long to relate the details of that chapter; I will be brief. Adrian Boult left in 1924 for Birmingham and we were looking for a young conductor to replace him. We found one by chance after hearing him conduct a composition of his own at one of the Proms—Malcolm Sargent. Once we had established the concerts in the centre of London we began building round the periphery. We started at the People's Palace so as to give poor children a chance to hear orchestral music. From the outset we wanted everybody to acquire the habit, not only of going to concerts, but also of paying for admission. We therefore made a charge of fourpence—not exactly expensive to hear a symphony orchestra conducted by Malcolm Sargent. Although we were playing to children who had never heard, let alone seen, a symphony orchestra, we played a strictly classical programme. The audience was so quiet and appreciative that those early concerts gave us enormous encouragement for the future, and we gradually built up a network round London, including Tottenham, West Ham, Wembley and other suburbs, seven in all. In the absence of concert halls we performed in cinemas, playing sometimes twice before lunch and again after lunch to satisfy the enormous local demand. One of our difficulties was that before every series Eugene Cruft, the leading double bass player and friend of all musicians, had to assemble an orchestra from scratch. This same situation led in 1932 to the foundation of the London Philharmonic Orchestra by Sir Thomas Beecham in conjunction with Samuel Courtauld and myself and other directors and financial backers.

EVENTUALLY we felt strong enough to extend the Robert Mayer Concerts beyond London and we started the invasion of Yorkshire, beginning with Leeds. This invited the envy of Huddersfield and Bradford, and we were glad to accommodate them. Finally we had seven centres in Yorkshire. We later added Newcastle, and then Derby and Coventry. Before the outbreak of the Second World War the score had risen from three concerts in London in 1923 to sixty-five in 1938 in twenty-five different centres. Looking back, I would say that this success was mainly due to three factors: our unwillingness to compromise on quality accepting only the best musicians and first-class programmes; our luck in finding Malcolm Sargent; and our ability to arouse the enthusiastic co-operation of the teachers, who brought hundreds of thousands of children to the concerts.

IN the 1930's, with our children growing up, we lived in the country, but we also had a house in St. John's Wood, where my wife gathered around her performers and composers, especially young ones. When the flood of Czech, Austrian and German refugees arrived in England, she discovered many musicians among them and invited them to come to our house for informal gatherings and to bring their instruments with them. This resulted in many wonderful gatherings, talks and musical evenings. Many other friends then living exiled in England, such as Carl Flesch, Stefan Zweig, Ernst Toller and Artur Schnabel, joined us for these evenings as well. I will never

Central Hall, Westminster

Orchestral Concerts

✦ ✦ FOR CHILDREN ✦ ✦

First Concert of Second Series

Reproduced by kind permission of Messrs. Rushworth & Dreaper.

Conductor, *Dr. MALCOLM SARGENT*
Leader, Mr. Samuel Kutcher

Saturday Morning
October 18th, 1924, at 11

Programme
and Notes

The second series of the concerts began on October 18th 1924. Dr. Malcolm Sargent became the resident conductor of the 'Symphony Orchestra for Children', composed of leading members of various London orchestras.

The first of many special concerts was the Beethoven Centenary celebration on March 19th 1927.

forget one of them when the Busch Quartet and Rudolph Serkin played the Dvôrak Piano Quintet and a young amateur violinist joined in, because everybody was welcome to participate. At the end of the evening one of our guests came up to Dorothy and myself and simply said *"Nun sind wir wieder Menschen"*—'Now we are human beings again'.

DIRECTING the Children's Concerts movement was a great strain, as I was also fully engaged in business. I had now reached the age of fifty and had to make up my mind whether to become a successful businessman or to extend my musical activities. I decided upon the latter course and in 1929, just before great depression set in, I gave up my position with the American firm. This meant giving up our car, but we did not give up our concerts. They weathered the storm, and in fact grew every year, as you have already heard, until the outbreak of the Second World War, when we were caught in the U.S.A. on holiday with our children. It was an awkward dilemma, but on the advice of the British Ambassador we stayed there, putting the children into school, while I worked at the British Consulate.

BEFORE the war we had from time to time lent our house in London for concerts in aid of the Save the Children Fund. It had a big brother in New York, the Save the Children Federation, and at the end of 1940 I offered my services as a dollar-a-year man, and was accepted. There I learned the technique of charity administration, including the art of economising on overhead expenses, which were in any case checked every month by a special Government department. A charity would be first warned and later put out of business if overheads were excessive. I have often thought when observing the wasteful way in which some British charities are run that we should imitate the American example.

WHEN the Federation became aware that my wife was a brilliant speaker they sent both of us on the road as lecturers. Two clergymen went ahead and "sold" us, as the

ROBERT MAYER
CONCERTS for CHILDREN

CENTRAL HALL
WESTMINSTER

Tuesday, 6th April 1937 at 11 a.m.

CORONATION CONCERT

LONDON SYMPHONY ORCHESTRA
Leader: W. H. READ, M.V.O.

Conductor:
DR. MALCOLM SARGENT

in the presence of

HER MAJESTY THE QUEEN
H.R.H. PRINCESS ELIZABETH
&
H.R.H. PRINCESS MARGARET ROSE

On Tuesday April 6th 1937 Her Majesty The Queen, HRH The Princess Elizabeth and HRH The Princess Margaret Rose attended the 'Coronation Concert' at the Central Hall, Westminster.

Central Hall, Westminster

ROBERT MAYER
Concerts *for* Children
(SIXTEENTH SEASON)

FIRST CONCERT

Saturday Morning, October 8th, 1938
Doors Open at 10.40 a.m.   Commence at 11 a.m. sharp

SOLOISTS :

JOHN BROWNLEE	IRENE EISINGER	DAVID FRANKLIN
ROY HENDERSON	AUDREY MILDMAY	HEDDLE NASH
	(of Glyndebourne Opera Company)	

London Symphony Orchestra
Leader : GEORGE STRATTON

CONDUCTOR :
EUGÈNE GOOSSENS

The London Symphony Orchestra played often for the Robert Mayer Concerts. On October 8th 1938 the conductor was Eugène Goossens and the soloists were members of the Glyndebourne Opera Company.

Central Hall, Westminster

ROBERT MAYER
Concerts *for* Children
(SIXTEENTH SEASON)

SECOND CONCERT

Saturday Morning, October 29th, 1938,
Doors Opened at 10.40 a.m.   Commence at 11 a.m. sharp

London Philharmonic Orchestra
(Leader : DAVID McCALLUM)

CONDUCTOR :
Sir THOMAS BEECHAM, Bart.
all of whom are generously giving their services

RENÉ LE ROY

The players of the London Philharmonic Orchestra were frequent visitors to the Children's Concerts. On October 29th 1938 they played under their conductor Sir Thomas Beecham.

29

LONDON MUSIC FESTIVAL

ROBERT MAYER
Concerts *for* Children
Patron : HER MAJESTY THE QUEEN

QUEEN'S HALL
Saturday, May 6th, 1939, at 11 a.m.

London Symphony Orchestra
Leader   GEORGE STRATTON

Conductor :
MALCOLM SARGENT

On Saturday May 6th 1939 Malcolm Sargent conducted the LSO for the last Robert Mayer Concert before the outbreak of World War II.

Americans so quaintly put it; they used our titles as a selling point, and I was somewhat embarrassed when I found myself billed one day as the 'Lord Mayor of London'. On our tour we experienced the extraordinary generosity of the American public; and we sent home large amounts of money, which were used principally for setting up residential nurseries for children whose fathers were in the army and mothers working in industry. After Pearl Harbour American mothers were becoming anxious about their own; so we ended our tour; my wife turned to hospital work and I resumed my activities with the Federation. Finally, in 1943 I returned home, leaving my wife behind, since she had to undergo a serious operation. I had to travel via Lisbon, where on my arrival I found hundreds of British children waiting for planes to take them home. To relieve their boredom I organised lessons in the morning, games in the afternoon and debates in the evenings, modelled on parliamentary procedure. For a short time I was a schoolmaster, a thrilling experience which I will not forget.

THE Germans were past masters in using music as a means of propaganda, and in our search for a similar propaganda weapon for use in the United States, we hit upon the idea of Glyndebourne, which had, of course, a unique reputation in the operatic world. The nearest American approach to an old world Sussex village was Williamsburg, an attractive reconstructed colonial town in Virginia, which was the apple of the eye of John D. Rockefeller, Junior. I managed to interest him in the idea of launching a second Glyndebourne Opera at Williamsburg and to get his promise to build a small opera house, which was to be ready in 1941. This happened during the "phoney war", when I found out at the Consulate that British exporters were keen to keep up their trade with America and to earn dollars. I secured the Ambassador's approval for the Glyndebourne idea and also for a new export scheme which I had evolved; and in January 1940 I sailed for England in order to crystallize both. I could make no progress with the business proposal, but I did get a lot of information from Rudolf Bing on how to run opera; so I went back to the U.S.A., travelling through Italy just before it entered the war, and tackled the Glyndebourne plan. I succeeded in obtaining the agreement of five unions and was negotiating with the most important of them, the Musicians' Union, when France fell, whereupon Mr. Rockefeller decided that he could not proceed with his side of the scheme.

ONCE more I was looking for a useful occupation, a task which was not made easier by the fact that I was over sixty years old. Marshall Field had started an organisation for bringing British children to America. I joined it, but it came unfortunately to an end when one hundred and thirty-four children were torpedoed in November 1940.

DURING my visits to Washington on leave, I had frequently been asked how the British were handling juvenile delinquency under war conditions. A look at the dictionary explained to me something of the meaning of that term, but I was more fully informed when on my return to England I called at the Home Office, where the official in charge was not satisfied merely to hand out dry statistics. He sent me to approved schools, juvenile courts and even borstals; and after a few months I felt that I could write a report and send it to New York. By chance the report fell into the hands of my friend Victor Gollancz, who decided to publish it; and to my utter surprise I had become an author, though only of a booklet entitled "Young people in Trouble". It went through three editions, and was at one time a textbook at the LSE. If I were not fully occupied now I would bring it up to date; intrinsically conditions here have not greatly changed, even in remand homes, which have been crying out for improvement all these years. Quite wrongly I was considered an expert in the field and as such I was invited by the Society of Friends, of which my wife had become a member, to tackle the problem of neglectful mothers, who under the law were often sent to prison. It seemed a particularly senseless way of treating them, since after they had been to prison they were generally worse mothers than before. I therefore gathered together a group of experts, induced the Home Secretary to provide some money, and

In 1923 Dorothy Moulton Mayer had reached a distinguished point in her career as singer of contemporary music.

Together with his wife, Robert Mayer started the Concerts for Children in 1923.

Until the Second World War, Malcolm Sargent was the regular conductor at the Children's Concerts. Here he discusses one of the works to be performed with (left to right) S. Kutcher, A. Pini, V. Watson, (Dr. Sargent), L. Goossens and Sir Robert Mayer. Sir Robert's daughter Pauline stands behind Mr. Pini,

Her Majesty The Queen with Her Royal Highness The Princess
Elizabeth at the Coronation Concert in 1937.

The Patron of the Robert Mayer Concerts, Her Majesty Queen Elizabeth The Queen Mother, brought Prince Charles, now the President of YOUTH & MUSIC, to his first concert in 1953.

Sir Robert's 90th birthday was celebrated in the Royal Festival Hall in the gracious presence of Her Majesty The Queen.

Lady Mayer with Sir Robert after the investiture during which Her Majesty The Queen had made him a member of the Order of Companions of Honour.

The Joint-Chairmen of *Youth & Music,* Sir Robert Mayer and the Earl of Drogheda (on the right), introduce officers of the International Federation *Jeunesses Musicales* to *Y & M* President, His Royal Highness The Prince of Wales. The occasion was a Henry Wood Promenade Concert shortly after Sir Robert's 99th birthday.

Sir Robert; how cartoonists have seen him.

On the eve of his 100th birthday Sir Robert presented a bust of himself to the BBC. The bust, sculpted by Hans Feibusch, was installed in the governors' dining-room at Broadcasting House.

Sir Hugh Casson, President of the Royal Academy, made this drawing of Sir Robert in February 1978.

YOUNG PEOPLE IN TROUBLE by SIR ROBERT MAYER · 2/6 net V.G

YOUNG PEOPLE IN TROUBLE

An outline survey of the methods and machinery by which society attempts to deal with the problems of juvenile delinquency in Britain

by

SIR ROBERT MAYER

Victor Gollancz was the first publisher to recognize the problems of juvenile delinquency the post war year might present. In 1945 he published Sir Rober Mayer's report on the subject for the Home Office. For some years this was the only authoritative survey on the treatment of juvenile delinquency in Britain.

42

founded the Elizabeth Fry Foundation to deal with the problem more sensibly. Owing to a technicality with which I will not bore you, the whole thing had to be dropped and the funds handed back to the Friends.

IN describing my charity work in the U.S.A. I should have mentioned the imaginative scheme whereby a million workers had one dollar deducted every month from their wages and transmitted to England for the benefit of needy children. When the war was over I enquired of the TUC how they proposed to reciprocate, a question which had not occured to them, evidently on the principle that it was more blessed to receive than to give. At that time I had discovered that in drawing up the Fulbright Bill, provisions for Americans to study in Europe included all types of students except those interested in further education. To remedy that situation, I founded the Transatlantic Foundation, designed to provide yearly scholarships at Ruskin College, Oxford, for young Americans drawn from the labour movement. Just because I happened not to be a socialist I found it easier to make out a case which convinced Ernest Bevin and the TUC of the value of the Foundation, and they joined in the scheme as partners. The scheme had always been intended to work both ways; but although the leaders of AFL and CIO, the American Unions, had promised to make it a two-way traffic, after eleven years they failed to do so. Although we had achieved good results, and even marriages between some of the American students, who evidently became victims of Oxford's amorous climate, the TUC and I decided finally to put the Foundation into cold storage, where it rests at present.

MY excursion into the student world brought me into contact with World University Service; I was offered the position of Honorary Treasurer, which I accepted. It opened up for me a new and interesting world, though addiction to the committee system resulted often in slow action and compromise, which were not to my liking. However, the managing group tolerated my non-academic mentality, and we worked happily together for ten years, until the 1956 crisis in Hungary gave us an opportunity for proving the real value of our organisation. We were the first to rescue hundreds of Hungarian students who wanted to continue their studies in non-academic professions. With the help of funds from the Government and the Lord Mayor of London, we were able to start them on a new life in England.

THIS seemed the appropriate moment to return to my first real love: music, and especially concerts for children. For a considerable time I had been plagued with an ever-recurrent concern to do something musically for young people who had left school, something along the lines of our own Children's Concerts. While considering various possibilities I got in touch with *Jeunesses Musicales,* a new movement which had been started on the continent during the war to encourage young people up to twenty-five, or even beyond, to go to concerts. It seemed to complement what we had been doing. We had left off at the adolescent stage, which was where they started. I therefore made attempts to start something similar in England; but they proved abortive until February 1954, when I managed to get various institutions working in the sphere of music and youth to come together at the Arts Council. This was the birth of Youth and Music, the counterpart of *Jeunesses Musicales.* The participants at the ceremony were scarcely a band of loving brothers, nor did they turn into fairy godmothers to the new-born baby, which was a slow developer. However, after two years we started a series of Youth Concerts at the Festival Hall, conducted by Norman Del Mar, which were originally meant primarily for the tens of thousands of members of youth clubs. It was impossible to attract them; "not for the likes of us" was the verdict given by the youth club leaders, with whom I had many meetings at my house in an attempt to over-come what was either an inferiority complex or an unfortunate result of the spirit prevailing in the sec-ondary modern schools, now absorbed into our comp-rehensive system. I had to abandon the idea of youth clubs, and canvassed people employed in commerce. In my innocence I thought they would rush at the chance of obtaining concert tickets at much reduced prices. What happened in fact was that the firms bought the blocks of tickets we offered them and then, taking the line of least resistance, charged up the cost to office expenses and practically gave the tickets away free. The purpose of the exercise was exactly the opposite. It was to ensure that these young people continued the habit of concert-going they had acquired earlier when they attended children's concerts. There was no other choice for me than to include schools also in our Youth and Music scheme and in fact to prepare children while at school for their after-school life. The Newsom Report had pointed to that very thing: the need to build a bridge between school and non-school life; and that's exactly what we did. One often wonders about the curious fact that such reports are prepared, at great trouble and expense, and contain valuable recommendations, yet are seldom ever acted upon.

THE fairy godmother must have been in hiding after 1954; but she turned up five years later when I discovered by chance that Sadler's Wells Opera, then in Rosebery Avenue, was closed to the public on Monday nights. I had never understood why opera was practically ignored in musical education. When you mention music to an educator he only thinks of concerts. I now saw a chance of remedying this situation by buying evenings of Sadler's Wells Opera exclusively for Youth and Music. It was a risky undertaking to buy four evenings, and the problem was how to fill the theatre. An intensive campaign, which this time included schools, proved unexpectedly fruitful. We sold all season tickets for the four nights. On the first night the enthusiasm was overwhelming, although, as shown by research, 97% of the audience had never been to an opera before. It proved the nonsense of saying that the English are not opera-minded. They do not lack interest in opera; they lack opportunities for hearing it. This innovation opened a new chapter in the history of Youth and Music, especially after we took in Covent Garden too; it was in fact the beginning of a remarkable expansion.

EVEN before this occurred we had a foretaste of things to come. In 1958 the Government had undertaken to participate in the International Festival of Youth Orchestras which was to be held as part of the Brussels World Fair, and asked us to implement that commitment at their expense. This was too good to be true. Needless to say, I took full advantage of the offer, making up an orchestra of students drawn from sixteen music and other colleges in London, Manchester, Glasgow, Cardiff, in fact, from all over Great Britain. It was conducted by Alexander Gibson. The Americans had sent to the Festival the Juillard School Orchestra, which consisted of professionals, and other countries sent similar bodies. When our turn came to perform we could truthfully announce that our orchestra had only come into being six days before. Whether for this or another reason, we received more applause than anybody else. We could show that Britain was a leader in student and youth orchestras. Thereupon we were inundated with invitations from other countries members of the Federation *Jeunesses Musicales,* to which Youth and Music had become affiliated. We chose Austria in preference to the others and in 1959 gave three concerts in Vienna which literally shook that old citadel of music. In the following year we sent three orchestras to Bayreuth, one of them led by John Georgiadis, the present leader of the London Symphony Orchestra.

AND so we progressed and began to see the musical scene in Britain as a whole, which meant that we had not only to create new audiences, but to work also for performers, both professional and amateur. We first turned to country and school youth orchestras, selecting among the large numbers that exist up and down the country, the very best and then collaborating with them in arranging visits abroad and appearances at home. For instance, more recently we sent a prominent orchestra to the Karajan Festival in Berlin, while another played at the Royal Festival Hall in aid of the Save the Children Fund.

NOR did we overlook the importance of trying to help outstanding young soloists, whose careers can be vitally affected by successes at international competitions. We therefore evolved a scheme whereby panels of eminent musicians audition and select performers who seem capable of winning prizes at competitions. For those selected we then provide pre-competition concerts in London and travel costs, and prize-winners' concerts for those who actually win. In 1970 we sent eighteen candidates, of whom one won the Tchaikovsky Competition in Moscow. This year sixteen were entered for competitions, four securing top prizes. Before we started this scheme the situation was most unsatisfactory: young soloists entered competitions who had no business to do so; they did no good either to themselves or to the prestige abroad of British music. We are glad to think that sense and order have been established and that we now possess the machinery for handling kindred propositions. For instance, we administer the Leverhulme Foundation scholarships for study adroad, and other awards enabling students to attend Tanglewood, the Rudolph Serkin and other summer schools.

IN conclusion may I say this: my Tolstoyan puritanism created in me from adolescence onwards a sense of duty to society which later I was able to fulfil through service to music. In this task I was greatly helped by my wife, and to some extent by Artur Schnabel, both being imbued with the spirit of non-compromise, an attribute particularly needed just now when the maintenance of real values is not always easy, although I wonder whether a measure of compromise is not perhaps at times unavoidable in this imperfect world if one wants to serve a great cause effectively. The outstanding achievement of the Robert Mayer Concerts for Children lies probably in the fact that after fifty years it has proved possible to build up a tradition among hundreds of schools which will persist and affect an ever-increasing number of young people. What has been possible in primary and preparatory schools should not be impossible in secondary schools, although the mentality of adolescents and the overwhelming importance attached by schools and society to examinations must create obvious difficulties. Young people who have left school and are now in business should, in theory, be as keen to take advantage of the benefits offered by Youth and Music as those who are still in school or attend the Children's Concerts. In practice this is unfortunately not the case. Since their elders in business lacked the opportunities which their children are now being given, music has never become sufficiently meaningful to them. Hence, they do not give a lead to their employees. However, Youth and Music has taken roots sufficiently both in London and outside, to enable it to grow, just as the Concerts for Children have done.

I WAS lucky to have entered public musical life in Britain when the tide was in my favour, and to participate in the flowering process which all of us are now witnessing. It begins to look as if the decline in Britain's political and economic power may coincide with her emergence as musically the most prominent nation. Such counter-balancing phenomena have often happened in past history. Today London is probably the most vital musical city in the world: witness its wide range of operatic and concert performances, the Proms, and not least, the enthusiastic participation of youth in musical activities. In addition, our musical institutions are modernising their structures, and this will strengthen London's position as a centre of learning. At the same time, opera companies, art centres and music schools are gradually growing up in other parts of the country. I am convinced that with vision, planning and co-operation, Britain's position, not only in the new Europe, but in the world generally, can become unassailable.

FANFARE FOR EUROPE

Youth & Music Concert
Royal Festival Hall
13th January, 1973

Britain's entry into the European Community was celebrated by *Youth & Music* with a Gala Concert for Young People. Colin Davis conducted the LSO in a programme of works by eminent British composers.

Two organisations which have done much to stimulate the increasing love and understanding of music in this country are celebrating their Golden Jubilee this season: the British Broadcasting Corporation and the Robert Mayer Concerts.

The first "Orchestral Concerts for Children" took place in the spring of 1923. Some of those in this hall today, fifty years later, are probably the grandchildren of people who heard those first concerts.

Throughout those fifty years, to the benefit of successive generations of audiences, Sir Robert Mayer and Lady Mayer have supported and guided these concerts, with the enthusiastic cooperation of a succession of distinguished conductors — there must be many here today who think especially of Malcolm Sargent, who conducted the concerts from 1924 to 1939.

These concerts have not been by any means the only way in which Sir Robert and Lady Mayer have contributed to the musical life of this country. They have created Youth and Music, a flourishing organisation which provides greater musical opportunities for young people in schools and in employment. And there are many young musicians, professional and amateur, who have reason to be grateful for their support and generosity in a variety of activities.

In this work for music in Britain, Sir Robert has, I know, been inspired by his own love of music and by his faith in Britain's musicality. That faith has been supported by the means to help, and by the vision, the alertness, and the practical good sense which characterise all he does and enable him to know how best to direct his help.

This Jubilee is indeed an occasion for celebration; but it is also an opportunity for all of us who love music, and set store by the increase of musical appreciation and activity in Britain, to express to Sir Robert and Lady Mayer our most grateful thanks for what they have done and are doing, and our warmest good wishes to them both.

Edward Heath

MINE is a one-tracked mind. I am vitally interested in causes which must often be of little interest to those on whom I am inflicting my views, in the hope that they will be accepted. My apparent selfishness is, I hope, lessened by the fact that I am concerned with an idea, something much bigger than myself. It was a mere coincidence that two friends kept a record of my improvised address delivered eight years ago which led to the publication of this book, *My First Hundred Years,* and in the second place my being urged to write my biography. The nearest I came to doing so was in 1967, when my wife and I flirted with writing *Double Concerto.* But my wife was a very private person, and there were other reasons for the world being deprived of a potential masterpiece.

I now endeavour to bring the story up to date by sketching a few outstanding events which occurred in my life from 1971 to 1979. First came a letter from Prime Minister Edward Heath, the most genuine and ardent music lover among the politicians of this century. He enquired whether he might advise the Queen to confer upon me the Order of the Companions of Honour. After consulting my life-long partner, my wife, I accepted with deep gratitude and with pride, which was shared by my children.

I cannot claim to be an expert on the question of honours. Some countries which have investigated this practice have decided against its adoption. Our society still seems to favour a kind of Greek moderation which runs counter to the mentality and attitude of many other countries. Broadly our honours system symbolises public recognition of merit which must surely be right. I would not wish to criticize the system. In any case I could not do so as the modus operandi is shrouded in mystery to ordinary mortals.

The day that the Queen conferred the decoration on me will always live in my memory. She granted me a half hour audience in a relaxed atmosphere. You will be scarcely surprised that I seized the opportunity of reporting to Her Majesty, on (to borrow an Americanism), the happy musical State of the Union.

On April 14th 1973 Her Majesty Queen Elizabeth The Queen Mother, Patron of the Robert Mayer Concerts, presided over the Golden Jubilee Concert at the Royal Festival Hall.

At about the same time my family met in order to discuss the future of the Children's Concerts (whose name was altered to Robert Mayer Concerts as people aged eleven or twelve years no longer wished to be called children). Our son and daughter are extremely busy people, and could not possibly add to their commitments. Moreover the change in social conditions prevented them from continuing the financial patronage which we were proud to extend to the movement ever since its inception. We suddenly thought of the B.B.C., which had years ago taken over the Proms, which are also a national, but far bigger movement. Hundreds of schools had become our faithful followers, and they were willing to transfer their loyalty to the world's leading broadcasting service. The pact between us and the B.B.C. was solemnised at a luncheon given by the Board who felt certain that the Concerts would be continued in the same spirit in which we had founded and administered them.

I HAVE always kept out of domestic politics. My business is music. One cannot serve two masters. That was one of the reasons why I gave up my career in business. This did not, however, impede my endeavours to raise my sights. Thus I became a convinced European. To translate my feelings into attempted action, I suggested to Mr. Heath that Britain's entry into the Common Market should be celebrated musically. Lord Eccles, the Minister of the Arts, entered into the picture though the matter was finally referred to that remarkable man in our midst in whose hands so many wires meet, Lord Goodman. With handsome Government support, a committee evolved, 'Fanfare for Europe', which planned on a vastly comprehensive scale: it included not only opera, ballet, concerts, but also the various facets of drama and visual arts, presented in different parts of the country as well as London. The ten days national festival occurred in January 1973.

Later I was to be implicated again in the Common Market though only to a very modest extent. Six months before the Referendum in 1974, like innumerable others, I offered my services to 'Britain in Europe' which was an organisation typically British: as far as I could see, the heads were men, some of whom had retired from active service. The actual work appeared to be carried on largely by women who, though unpaid, were singularly enthusiastic. It made me wonder once more about the community's curious attitude to women. We revere a woman who occupies a position of supreme importance, our Queen. We assign to women the grave responsibilities attached to Ministers of the Crown, and so on, and yet we cannot get rid of prejudices, which seem nonsensical in the present day. If further proof were needed, it was supplied abundantly during the first World War when women served society in many directions at least as well as men. In the Referendum campaign I wished to address women, who might be possibly persuaded by a layman that the issue was much bigger than the price of butter: in the new Europe-in-the-making, war was far more unlikely than it had been in the past. Developments before the Referendum deprived me of the chance of mounting, for the only time in my life, the political hustings. I was clearly meant to stick to my trade and to avoid excursions into spheres operated to better advantage by others.

In any case, I had to concentrate on my work of musical planning, which was difficult for me as my wife's health made me desperately anxious. She was relieved from agonising pain in April 1974 when she left this life for another existence, possessed of faith and incredible courage. Ours was a real partnership, extending over sixty years. Driven by humanity, ideals, curiosity, she was unusually inventive. I am more gifted in organisation and in realising visions. Thus we complemented each other. In addition we were united in detesting sham and compromise.

We live at a time when the virtue of action is endangered by lack of self-reliance and faith. It seems to me that especially in a country like ours, which is practically devoid of natural resources, salvation cannot come from bureaucracy, but from confidence in ourselves, initiative and action.

TO return to my subject, the latter philosophy forms the basis of Youth & Music, which has undergone a notable change since I referred to it in my earlier remarks. In its early years it could not help being a one-man-show. Now it is a well-constituted body, with a management committee of able individuals. It is recognised as the unifying and a creative force in its special field. For many years the financial responsibility was mine. Now we can look upon the Arts Council and the Greater

London Council as main supporters. Quite recently, thanks to Lord Drogheda, and Lois Sieff, who initiated a Concert celebrating the 21st Birthday of Youth and Music, and the ninety-sixth of its founder, the private sector has joined the roster of patrons: more than 100 business and other institutions have combined to increase our reserves. With the fortunate advent of my very dear friend Lord Drogheda as my colleague, the problem of Y & M's continuity has been solved. A movement like ours cannot remain static: in spite of the country's present financial crisis, it is consistently expanding; the ordinary running of the business being in the capable hands of our Hon. Treasurer, John Denison, our administrator, Alan Fluck, our secretary, Elsa Johnston, and our PRO, Christopher Evans. They in turn have the benefit of the counsel of the Trustees and the Board: Lois Sieff, Albert Frost, Richard Baker, Michael Kaye, my son Adrian Mayer, Michael Rubinstein, and my daughter Pauline Samuelson. Our operations fit into the policies of the Arts Council and of the Regional Arts Associations with whom Y & M is operating.

Looking ahead, and especially at the New Europe, one of the links unifying the ten countries might well be music; in that case, Britain, thanks to its exemplary national structure, should be in the best position to provide leadership.

A beginning was made when Mr. Edward Heath and the ever-inventive Mrs. Bryer founded the EEC Orchestra, which became a reality in 1978; a young companion to the well-seasoned World Youth Orchestra which has functioned to good purpose under the aegis of the International Federation of Jeunesses Musicales and, so far, the generous patronage of the Canadian Government.

A FTER the end of the first World War, when I was still active in the metal and mining business, my wife and I lived in the United States of America. We loved it. Besides, the example of the American Walter Damrosch, the innovator of children's concerts, inspired my wife with an idea which was to change our lives completely. I felt that I owed a debt to that great country which I could hope to repay by making known to some of its key people in musical life how we in Britain have built miraculously well since 1945. With the collaboration of the British Council

YOUTH & MUSIC
GALA CONCERT

CELEBRATING THE

21st BIRTHDAY OF YOUTH AND MUSIC

AND THE

96th BIRTHDAY OF SIR ROBERT MAYER

THURSDAY, OCTOBER 23rd 1975

Greater London Council
Royal Festival Hall

DIRECTOR: JOHN DENISON CBE

and the Foreign Office it was possible three years ago to organise a coast-to-coast lecture tour. In it I did not presume to counsel that great country on how to run 'musical America'; I merely described our activities. Fortunately it proved possible to link up my lectures with a series of concerts by the London Schools Symphony Orchestra which was conducted by that singularly gifted twenty one year old Simon Rattle. We were able to demonstrate to admiring American audiences the high standard of playing by young British music makers.

This was our first attempt at real Anglo-American musical links. My dream has long been to create a common pool into which Britain could pour valuable experience which was gained from building our present structure; America could contribute her youth, wealth and her great potentials which, so far, have not been explored into a coordinated way. There is no limit to those potentials and an Anglo-American musical force would be irresistible.

I HAVE dreamt since my youth that divine providence will grant me the privilege of dying in harness. Of course I cannot tell you when you will read my obituary notice, which will doubtless be overkind, but in the meantime I can only promise myself and warn you that I will carry on my work which exists for the benefit of our youth and which tries to replace prevailing violence and ugliness by harmony and beauty.

THE ANATOMY
OF A MIRACLE

Campbell-Orde Memorial Lecture 1972

In calling this lecture 'The Anatomy of a Miracle', I am using the word Miracle in a limited, colloquial sense. A miracle in that sense is something everybody knows can't happen and won't. But it does happen. And we're all very stunned and bewildered and try to work out how it came about. It's this working-out process that I call the Anatomy.

Now the Miracle I want to talk about to-night is Britain's vast Musical Awakening, Musical Explosion, Musical Eruption—call it what you like, so long as your words are emphatic enough. It so happens that this Miracle started in the mid-1890s, precisely the time when as a very young man, I came from Germany and settled in London. There were at that time two main concert halls in London. One was the St. James's Hall, which stood on a site between Regent Street and Piccadilly. On Saturdays and Mondays there were so-called Pop Concerts there—chamber music of the highest classical quality led by the famous Joseph Joachim. Then there was the Queen's Hall, almost brand new when I heard my first Promenade Concert there. And this is where the Miracle really starts.

For it is the Proms, rather than any other concert series, whether in the flesh or over the air, which sensitised generation after generation of English listeners, increasing their number and opening their ears to musical styles, forms and idioms. I've got to admit that the Miracle didn't start overnight with the first Prom. The early Henry Wood programmes were apt to be of the ragbag type. Twenty items or more, not counting encores: The *Lost Chord,* Schubert's *Serenade* and *Love's Old Sweet Song* were in great demand as cornet solos. There were trombone quartets, post-horn gallops, excruciatingly sentimental ballads and 'grand selections' from *Carmen, Rigoletto,* and Gilbert and Sullivan. But the standard symphonic classics, starting in some cases as one-movement excerpts, quickly took root. There were Wagner 'first halves' and Beethoven 'first halves'. Then complete Wagner nights and complete Beethoven nights. And so on. Wood was soon giving us 'difficult' or newish music from Russia and Germany. The tonepoems of Richard Strauss, for example. Arnold Schoenberg, even. Wood put on Schoenberg's Five Orchestral Pieces before the first world war. The critics were flabbergasted. There were hisses. Moussorgsky and Rimsky-Korsakov came our way — and more startling than these, Igor Stravinsky. Nor must I forget the French. Debussy and Ravel swam into our ken like new worlds. In those days we paid a shilling for standing places down in the arena. People used to ask how on earth, at such prices, Wood made the Proms pay their way. The answer is simple. They didn't pay their way. They lost something like £2,000 a season at first. Around 1900 £2,000 was *real* money. In those days there were no State subventions to fall back on. For ten years the Proms deficits were met by a banker, namely, Edgar Speyer. Speyer's passion for music and his devotion to philanthropic causes were profound, though his work for the Queen's Hall and the Proms is not even noticed in any edition of Grove's Dictionary. The pioneer's lot has never been a happy one.

Those were times when ambitious music-making depended more often than not upon some individual. Let us call him Mr. Maecenas. The two decades preceding the first world war were Mr. Maecenas's heyday, although he occasionally popped up again to good purpose during the 1920s and 1930s. A roughly parallel role to that of Sir Edgar Speyer was played in New York by another banker, Otto Hermann Kahn who, like myself, had been born and bred in Mannheim, and who became the driving force of the Metropolitan Opera Company in New York. Here in England we had a Mr. Maecenas who not only lavished a private fortune on symphonic music and opera, but also conducted and produced the stuff, with subtle art and a sort of sublime fury. I refer, of course, to the incomparable Thomas Beecham. Before Beecham descended on the Royal Opera, Covent Garden, people used to go there in the main, to hear the world's great voices. For that was the golden age of The Voice. Some people, indeed, regarded Voices as more important than the music they sang. Beecham made short work of such heresies. He put on and conducted two highly controversial operas by Richard Strauss—*Salome* and *Elektra*—with a contagious conviction and zeal that converted musical London well nigh overnight to music which had hitherto been regarded as above its head. In the concert hall he was equally resolute and daring, as proved, for instance, by his unveiling of Frederick Delius's art which was unknown until then. All in all, Beecham takes high rank among those magical talents that are destined to resensitise and school the ears and musical minds of the multitudes. The Diaghilev ballet seasons which he sponsored before the first world war converted a privileged generation to the revolutionary marvels of *Firebird, Petrushka, The Rite of Spring* and much else. A generation or two earlier a portentous German writer had described England as 'Das Land ohne Musik'—the land without music. Superficially there was something in this gibe. But how can a people be described as musicless who produced not only the Elizabethan madrigalists, but also one of the greatest composers of all times—Henry Purcell? Moreover, from end to end of England, in the great Gothic Cathedrals, in most remote village churches, people sang. There were no better choirs in the world than those in Yorkshire or in London. But because the sophisticated continental taste of the time was for chamber or orchestral music these facts were not assessed at anything like their right value. Beecham was one prominent among those who laid the foundation on which much has risen that would have surprised, while gratifying, even him.

An early hint of great things to come was the Beecham

Symphony Orchestra: the first English orchestra to reach anything like the virtuoso class. Beecham founded it in 1906. Six years later it was chosen by Diaghilev to accompany an illustrious ballet season of his in Berlin at the Kroll Opera House. Kaiser Wilhelm attended several of the performances. At last an English Orchestra had found a place on the Continental map. That in itself was an indication of the Miracle.

We must remember that during my early years in London the city hadn't a single permanent orchestra in the current meaning of that phrase. To-day we have five! Players were at that time engaged on an *ad hoc basis*. This applied even to the orchestra that played for the venerable Philharmonic Society. Around the turn of the century orchestral work in general was rough and ready, sometimes abysmal. For his Proms, Henry Wood made do with three morning rehearsals, nine hours in all, for every six concerts. Once a piece had been rehearsed it was not readily dropped. There were popular overtures by, and excerpts from, Wagner, Tchaikovsky, Grieg and Schubert that were repeated three or four times in a single season. Orchestral players were so poorly paid that often a man might attend morning rehearsal and, if offered a more profitable job in the meantime, absent himself 'on the night', sending a deputy in his place. I remember an occasion when Wood, at a morning Prom rehearsal, was confronted by an orchestra with seventy faces in it which he had never seen before. His orchestra, or nearly all of it, had been casually booked for some provincial festival starting on the same day. Conditions prevailing then seem incredible to-day.

The first world war brought a big change. There had been a high proportion of Germanic players in London orchestras and leading provincial ones. Early in August 1914 they disappeared overnight. Their places were taken by English musicians either under or over military age. The lesson which gradually dawned upon us was that we could increase the number of our English orchestras *and* man them

64

with homegrown, English talent. What didn't dawn on us until decades later was that the orchestras thus recruited would, through world tours and prestigeous gramophone recordings in a highly competitive market, achieve world fame and the highest international playing standards.

The first world war, indeed, taught us other lessons besides musical ones. The outbreak of that war found this country shockingly unprepared in all directions—industrially as well as militarily. We had imported not only much of our food, but also nearly all the chemicals, dyes, minerals and other commodities essential to a society like ours. To survive during the war we were obliged to produce these commodities ourselves. This meant the beginning of a new Industrial Britain which led in time to such giant concerns as Imperial Chemical Industries—and which proved that the people of Britain had the energy, initiative and intelligence to rely on their own strength. The way in which we rose to the occasion industrially was matched by what happened musically.

As soon as the war began, Covent Garden had to close down. The glamorous trade of Great Voice imports from the ends of the earth folded for 'the duration'. The sequel would have been something like silence but for Beecham. In 1915 he got together a company of forty or more principal singers, practically all of them British. In various London theatres, as well as in Manchester, he put on highly original seasons of opera in English, initiating packed audiences, to stylish and often powerful productions of such unhackneyed things as *Boris Godounov,* Puccini's *Manon Lescaut, Tristan and Isolde,* Gounod's *Romeo and Juliet,* Charpentier's *Louise,* three other Russian pieces—*Ivan the Terrible, Khovantachina, The Golden Cockrel*—and above all, Verdi's *Otello.* I say 'above all' in this case because, as very few people in this audience will remember, Otello was sung by the great Frank Mullings, an actor-singer of genius. Mullings's stage career was a relatively short one. It is safe to say, I think, that if it hadn't been for Beecham little would have been heard of him. The same goes for the other eminent singers who got their chance with the Beecham Opera and with its short-lived successor, the British National Opera Company. Their achievements were quite beyond the dreams of such other homegrown outfits as the Carl Rosa and Joseph O'Mara companies and Lilian Baylis's 'opera on a shoestring' at the Old Vic theatre in the Waterloo Road. Throughout the ages only a small percentage of citizens in any community are really interested in art, be it music or any other. On this basis Beecham proved abundantly that among the English there are proportionately as many with a strong natural appetite for opera and a natural capacity for performing it as you'll find in any country. All that our potential audiences needed was the opportunity of seeing and hearing opera.

Unfortunately, it is the costliest of all the theatrical arts. In those days it was assumed that it would go on being paid for out of the pocket of this Mr. Maecenas and that the idea of setting up national opera companies in Britain and subsidising them from taxes and rates on the Continental model was dismissed as, well, silly. By the end of the 1914 war Beecham had dropped clean out of the Maecenas class. He had spent just about the whole of his share in the Beecham family fortune and was in trouble with his creditors. To get money for a continuation of his operatic enterprises he went to the country rather in the manner of a Prime Minister out for re-election. Opera lovers at large were asked to pay a pound down and annual subscriptions of ten shillings a year, thus becoming members of what Beecham grandly called the Imperial League of Opera. Yet, despite Beecham's wit and fiery oratory, the Imperial League flopped—largely because many people were put off by Beecham's attitude as a campaigner. To call people dumb-heads and philistines was hardly the way to get money out of them. Sir Hugh Allen, who was then the head of the Royal College of Music, put it this way: 'There are some people who slap you in the face and ask for half-a-crown. Beecham slaps you in the face and asks for a five pound note!'

Yet, for all his unlucky way of handling matters, Beecham survived and formidably helped the great Miracle along. Apart, perhaps, from the Halle Orchestra in the North, we then had only one Orchestra of rising prestige and genuine stability. That was the BBC Symphony Orchestra, the creation (in effect) of the BBC's director-general, John Reith. Reith was himself no musician. He wasn't very much interested in music. But he knew that music had required patronage throughout the ages. Being a man of determination and iron convictions, he laid down a massive policy. The BBC was to become not just a purveyor of music, but the leader of music. And its leadership was to cover not only the Beethovens, the Mozarts, the Handels and the Brahmses. It was to present also contemporary works—which had as little popular appeal then as they have to-day. As evidence of his farsightedness we need only remember the backing he gave to the late Edward Clark, a young conductor whose championing of Schoenberg and other living masters gave a touch of its own to musical broadcasting in the 1930s and later. Many have testified quite recently to Reith's rare vision. It was he who laid the foundations of a musical structure which is a matter of marvel and envy throughout the world.

My wife and I first met Reith when he came to one of our children's concerts, soon after we started them at the Central Hall, Westminster. Reith looked at the orchestra and asked what its name was. I explained that it was a scratch orchestra and had to be got together for each Concert. I added that there was only one permanent orchestra in London, and that was the BBC's. I am talking now of 1924. "Nonsense!", said Reith. "You shall have mine." A typically generous proposal. Unfortunately it had to be dropped. It turned out that the BBC Orchestra was busy every Saturday morning—which was the morning our own concerts were held. Eight years afterwards Adrian Boult, who was then the BBC's director of music, told us that certain members intended launching children's concerts under BBC auspices. In those far-off days all innovations had to be approved by Reith. On this occasion he himself drew up the directive. He laid it down as a prior condition that the new project must not damage our movement in any way, and that the BBC should, on the contrary, take steps to help it along. As a result of this the BBC, when they started children's concerts, actually did so under my name. What is more, the announcer used to urge young listeners to come to our concerts at the Central Hall if they wanted to hear 'the real thing'. Can you imagine anything similar happening to-day? Well, that was Reith. I'm afraid you'll not see his like again in your lifetime. One last thought on this theme. It was the Reith regime that regalvanised the Henry Wood Proms. Having been financially ailing for years, the Proms were taken over by the BBC in 1930 and became one of the BBC Symphony Orchestra's many thrones. Gradually other orchestras, playing under their own conductors, were invited to take part. Finally, Sir William Glock broadened the series immeasurably and turned them into an annual international festival, unprecedented in magnitude and splendour. Nothing like the Proms exist in any part of the world. But I have kept Beecham waiting in the wings. Back to the 1930s. No sooner was the BBC Symphony Orchestra well launched than Beecham decided it wasn't good enough and that he could do better. He and I had first met in 1931, when, as guarantors, we jointly made it possible for the Berlin Philharmonic Orchestra to tour England under Furtwangler, an event which not only gave great pleasure to music lovers, but served also to raise the sights of our own orchestral players. When Beecham stressed the need for another orchestra—to be named the London Philharmonic —which was to be established on a permanent basis, I helped in the realisation of the plan. Annual deficits were envisaged, of course. Samuel Courtauld and, to a modest extent, myself, undertook in substance to meet them. We organised plenty of work for the LPO. The Royal Philharmonic Society, the Royal Choral Society, the Courtauld-Sargent and likewise the Robert Mayer organisation—all undertook to employ the orchestra after it was formed. In this way an unusually strong basis was established for the orchestra, which gave its opening concert at the Queen's Hall forty years ago. Not only Britain, but the greater world of music had a new orchestra of newly-enrolled, newly-trained players. With Beecham at the helm, the LPO perfected its style, stoked its musical fires and quickly cemented its international reputation on the world gramophone recording market.

The interwar years were also formative British music in other directions. It was these years that witnessed the creation of the International Society for Contemporary Music. The I.S.C.M. was born in our house, with the celebrated musicologist, the late Edward J. Dent, and the octogenarian, Egon Wellesz—who made Oxford his home when Hitler invaded Austria—serving as midwives. The Society gave its inaugural concert in 1922 in Salzburg. Naturally I joined my wife on that occasion, when she sang music by Vaughan Williams, Bax, Goossens, Bliss and other contemporary British composers. She thus continued the recital work which she had begun soon after the first world war in Germany, Austria and Hungary, where public and professionals alike lived in abysmal ignorance of our music —they hardly knew, in fact, that we had any contemporary composers! Their ignorance derived largely from our own penchant for understatement and aversion to publicity. This penchant is a civilised quality *per se*. Nevertheless, it seems to me that in this highly competitive world, where publicity and overstatement abound, we must change our attitude somewhat or suffer the consequences.

My wife's travels on the Continent brought her into contact with prominent musicians in various countries whom she invited to stay with us when visiting London, a city where it was still possible to cultivate and keep open house for artists and friends. Our visitors' book dates back fifty years and shows as first entrant Bela Bartók.

Bartók played with a precise, steely touch and incredible force before a small spellbound audience. One of the

69

listeners marvelled, in fact, that the piano wasn't in bits at the end of it. Artur Schnabel, the pianist, was another visitor. Schnabel not only played after his own lofty, inimitable fashion, he also dreamed aloud. One thing about his dreams: they had a way of coming true. He told his hosts about an institution in Berlin known as the Volksbuehne, the people's theatre. The point of the Volksbuehne was that it put on high-quality concerts and plays for working-class audiences at very low prices, musicians and actors giving their services. Wouldn't it be a good thing to start something of the same sort in London? That was the question Schnabel put. It was soon answered. And in a practical way. The sequel to Schnabel's dream was the nine-year sequence of Courtauld-Sargent concerts at the Queen's Hall. The musical director of the series was a dynamic man called Malcolm Sargent about whom I will speak again in a minute. Some of the concerts were conducted by him. Most were allocated to celebrities from the Continent, including two names that were to resound more later on: Otto Klemperer and George Szell. Tickets were block-booked by big business firms and sold at concessions to their employees. There were annual deficits, of course. The bills were met by two of the dying species of Maecenas, Mr. and Mrs. Samuel Courtauld, who had similarly tided the Royal Opera over many a financial stile. The Courtauld-Sargent concerts made no concession whatever to lowbrow tastes. The slant was on the whole towards unfamiliar music, both old and 'contemporary'.

When describing the emergence of the LPO, I mentioned a title: the Robert Mayer Concerts. I trust you will not consider me immodest if I tell you something about these. They are not so much my brainchild as the brainchild of my wife, although the original idea came from the U.S.A. In fact, we started where New York left off. When we launched the concerts 50 years ago, children had scarcely ever heard, let alone *seen*, a symphony orchestra. We therefore started from scratch—which makes things easy in one sense, though we had a terrific struggle to convince people that children would be interested in first-class music performed by first-class orchestras. However, we are both inclined to take the line of most resistance. Furthermore, we had fanatical faith in the power of music. So we took up the challenge. After six years we had the movement firmly established in Greater London and could then extend it to other parts of the country. Immediately before the outbreak of the second world war the score was as follows: We had started in 1923 with three concerts a season in London, and during 15 years we had established 65 concerts in 25 different centres. From the outset our main aims were: First, to make children love music; Second, to get them into the habit of concert-going and paying for tickets. We succeeded in both directions and hundreds of thousands of young people had their first introduction to the magic of live symphony concerts. For much of that achievement we have to thank the fact that Malcolm Sargent was in charge of the London concerts during the interwar years. He was the ideal conductor and compere. Equally we must thank the very large number of teachers who shared our feeling that the enjoyment of music should no longer be considered the preserve of a privileged few; and that listening to, as well as making, music should be especially fostered among those who are still at the formative and therefore most easily influenced stage: namely, the young. After fifty years we can claim that hundreds of schools traditionally go to public symphony concerts and will continue doing so even though the founders will no longer be among them.

After the war schools started concerts in their own buildings—which is all to the good: but they must necessarily be given free of charge, as part of the curriculum. The danger about this is that on leaving school young people may automatically equate concerts with two things: something that is compulsory and something you get for nothing. The question is: Which of the two systems is the more constructive? Doubtless you can give your own reply. In any case our system requires public concert halls. These are sadly lacking even in large cities. It is to be hoped that this lack will breed discontent and thereby help to start reform and modernisation. There are at present far too many cities or regions devoid of concert halls and opera houses; from being undeveloped or under-developed communities, they must advance sufficiently to earn classification as developed communities. In Britain only London has reached that state. Are we to infer therefore that the citizens of Manchester, Birmingham, Glasgow and other leading cities are less musical than Londoners? This argument is manifestly absurd. The question arises, therefore, how to improve matters. A welcome beginning has been made by creating a chain of art centres which covers many regions. But I suggest that the real impetus must come from the citizens themselves and especially from YOUTH. Only they can put pressure on authority by demanding that they, too, may participate in Britain's glorious renaissance.

Another Miracle of the inter-war period was Glyndebourne Opera which was founded in 1934 by two Maecenases: John and Audrey Christie. Only an eccentric genius like John Christie could have had the imagination and audacity to build an opera house on his delightful estate situated near the Sussex Downs, and expect people to travel long distances to hear opera performed in a small theatre. But they did come and were rewarded by performances of the highest order, not only because the founders were perfectionists, but also the performing artists loved the novel idea of combining rehearsals which were organised irrespective of their length with the stay in a charming country house. Although the tickets were understandably expensive, yet the attraction was so great that even less pecunious members of the public were known to dig into their savings in order to make the pilgrimage to Glyndebourne. I happen to have a particular interest in it as I received during the war backing from Mr. D. Rockefeller, Junior, to take Glyndebourne to his cherished Williamsburg in Virginia. Unfortunately war developments prevented the idea from being ratified, and the project had never been revived since. In the meantime Glyndebourne, under the aegis of the founder's son, is carrying on and has, in fact, extended its usefulness by sending a touring company around the country.

The musical trail of the past was blazed by a whole chain of English talents and geniuses, not only by Henry Wood and Thomas Beecham, but also by Hamilton Harty in Manchester with his Halle orchestra; Adrian Boult; Malcolm Sargent; by Lilian Baylis, who transplanted her 'shoestring opera' from the Waterloo Road to its first seat of expansion and renown at Sadler's Wells in North London; and by a whole swarm of keen young solo players and orchestral players and amateur choirs and junior conductors and music-ologists and teachers and progressionists. It was a trail that led us through the second World War—with its attendant orchestral-concert boom that regularly packed concert halls and not a few vaudeville theatres throughout the land. Peace came, and at this point I must take you back for a minute to 1924 when the then Chancellor of the Exchequer, Philip Snowden, at the prompting of his wife, made a grant of £2,500 to Covent Garden. You would have expected that everybody concerned with music would have enthusiastically acclaimed a valuable precedent from which they all might hope to benefit. The contrary happened. Everybody was jealous and protested: why not me? As a result of this attitude and also in part because another Government came into power the following year, even this tiny grant was not renewed. During the subsequent twenty years a miracle which had been germinating—if miracles do germinate—suddenly blossomed, or, if you want a more powerful word—exploded. Let me tell you how the explosion happened. During the war the Council for the Encouragement of Music and the Arts—C.E.M.A. as it was known—had provided entertainment of all kinds for the armed forces. At the end of the war the Pilgrims Trust proposed that C.E.M.A. should be absorbed into a new organisation called

The Arts Council of Great Britain, whose purpose would be the strengthening of Britain's artistic life. Obviously the Council's terms of reference included the most comprehensive of the Arts: Music. First the Trust proposed a modest grant if the Treasury would do the same. The Government agreed. The Arts Council came into being with an initial Treasury grant of about £200,000. Whitehall and the Mother of Parliaments thus entered into the picture. As the time at my disposal is limited (fortunately for you) it is impossible for me to relate in detail the exciting story of the Arts Council's growth. Watching that growth from the start, I was particularly struck by the fact that the Council resisted all temptation to usurp or try to usurp the work of existing musical societies and institutions. They wisely limited themselves, on the contrary, to advice and financial help. During their twenty-six years existence they have served as a centre where wires met, and what had been a sporadic culture became a co-ordinated one.

To cut a long story short, the Arts Council receives for music in England now roughly £4½ million of which approximately £2½ million go to the two London Opera Houses. The rest is distributed to excellent constructive purposes among endless numbers of claimants—orchestras, opera companies, scholarships, provincial and amateur muisc-making societies, in fact, in all facets of musical life. The money is channelled from the Treasury to the Arts Council through another miraculous innovation dating from the 1960s when the Government created a new office, The Ministry with Responsibility for the Arts. We are indeed happy at the presence among us tonight of the present incumbent, Lord Eccles.

May I now return once more to the position of opera whose growth is, of course, of paramount importance.

History suggests that great foreign opera companies— resident ones, I mean—take anything from a quarter of a century to half a century to achieve ensemble styles and techniques on which genuine artistic ambience and tradition can be based. History also testifies that within 10 or 15 years Covent Garden became probably the most versatile and accomplished of all opera houses. If this does not amount to a Miracle, I don't know what will. Some part in the Miracle was played, it must be acknowledged, by foreign-born musical directors; in the sixties notably the fiery indefatigable George Solti who was fortunately backed to the hilt by the Covent Garden Board. In the operatic field, however, Covent Garden has not been the only big tree. There has been the sudden, opulent spread of Sadler's Wells Opera. From the Waterloo Road Lilian Baylis's company had moved long ago to Rosebery Avenue. Sadler's Wells, too puts on opera all the year around, sung in English by a company of British singers numerous enough to sustain provincial tours and prestigeous enough to be in demand on the Continent. Most people found Rosebery Avenue an awkward place to get to. They got there just the same. They were model audiences; intelligent and warmhearted. But the stage was cramped and ill-equipped. Four years ago the Company moved to The Coliseum, with its vast stage, vast auditorium and first-class West-End location. With this move another new chapter was added to the history of English opera.

It is time now to remember that the parallel orchestral growth has been as arresting in its way as operatic growth.

Let me therefore return to the days when Beecham launched the LPO. In those days London was ruled by the London County Council. In 1932 I went to the LCC and tried to convince them that, just as their opposite numbers in Berlin, Vienna and other capitals financially supported leading orchestras in those cities, so London should be proud to do the same for the new London Philharmonic. My interview with the Leader of the LCC was short and to the point. I was politely shown the door. It is wonderful to realise that in less than fifteen years the Miracle had signally changed the situation. At the end of the war London had two big orchestras, apart from the BBC Symphony Orchestra.

I have just told you about the London Philharmonic Orchestra. The other was the London Symphony Orchestra, dating back to 1904. The LSO, too, was self-governing. It had managed to survive for forty years although things were not always easy for them. On the Continent and elsewhere the greatest cities make do with two independent, permanent orchestras. It might have been expected that London would go on making do with two. The Miracle decided otherwise; it said, "Let there be four!". No sooner said than done. Beecham promptly founded the Royal Philharmonic and Walter Legge the Philharmonia. Both Orchestras stood on their own feet and paid their own way. Finally, a new dramtic situation developed. Some five years ago the Arts Council and the LCC's successor, the Greater London Council, working on a 50-50 basis, set up the London Orchestral Board, which has been subsidising the Big Four ever since. Local authorities generally are authorised to spend a tiny portion of their rate funds on the symphonic and other arts, under legislation that dates back to 1944. Sad to relate: very few of them have so far availed themselves of what they should consider to be an opportunity and a responsibility. One has only to think, to give just one example, of the cheese-paring attitude of Manchester's City Fathers to the Halle Orchestra during John Barbirolli's years there.

A few minutes ago I told you how the Miracle affected the GLC, which is, however, not the only pebble on the beach of public bodies which have joined the rank of patrons. We have also the City Corporation, which has drawn liberally upon its vast resources to provide the City with a real Arts Centre situated in the Barbican, where they are going to house the Guildhall School of Music, and a new Concert hall, with the London Symphony Orchestra as resident orchestra. The new City concert hall is especially needed, as the Royal Festival, Royal Albert and Queen Elizabeth halls are always, sometimes as much as two years, booked ahead; as also are the Fairfield halls, away out in

Croydon. The traffic congestion in central London, the unsatisfied appetite of the populace for orchestral fare, the expected invasion of orchestras from partners in the Common Market countries; these factors demand and justify the building of more concert halls. The Government rightly holds that responsibility for musical expansion should be shared by local authorities whose unsatisfactory mentality on such issues I have just described. This leaves a third member of the triumvirate: the sector of big-scale private finance. In this sector only a number of the Foundations have played an important part so far. In the USA leading industrial firms have used the medium of music for prestige purposes; and business concerns over here are beginning to take a leaf from their book. But by and large patronage from big business is as yet minimal. We need hardly be surprised at this, because most heads of firms grew up in an age when music played only an insignificant part in ordinary life.

You have patiently followed my attempt to point to the changes which have overtaken musical life. We must, however, face up to the fact that rather than make changes most people prefer to cling to old habits. The best hope of accelerating the tempo of expansion is to get to work on the young. I have already referred to my own endeavour to arouse the enthusiasm of children, though I have not yet described my efforts to influence similarly those who were approaching school-leaving age or who had already left school. To deal with adolescents and post-adolescents I founded Youth and Music eighteen years ago. At first it functioned only in the symphonic world. Later I added opera and gave the movement a new dimension. If you go to Covent Garden and the Coliseum you will often see friendly clusters of young people, running into many hundreds at a performance. These are members of Youth and Music who can buy tickets at much-reduced prices, thanks to the enlightened co-operation of the managements, who realise how important it is to build up audiences of the future. That is exactly the business of Youth and Music.

QUEEN ELIZABETH HALL

Sunday, October 25, 1970, at 3 p.m.

YOUTH & MUSIC

presents

JOHN LILL

FIRST PRIZE AND GOLD MEDAL

INTERNATIONAL TCHAIKOVSKY COMPETITION

MOSCOW 1970

Programme

Chaconne in D minor	**BACH, arr. BUSONI**
Sonatine	**RAVEL**
Sonata No. 7, Op.83	**PROKOFIEV**

INTERVAL

Sonata in F, Op. 54	**BEETHOVEN**
Variations and Fugue on a Theme by Handel	**BRAHMS**

However, our duties are not confined to creating audiences for opera. We do the same on an ever-increasing scale for concerts. And, to be constructive, in yet another way, we also help outstanding young performers by sending them abroad to take part in international competitions. At these, many of our candidates have been successful—to the benefit of their careers and Britain's musical prestige. As you may be aware, we had four first prize-winners last year and one of our candidates won the much-coveted Tchaikovsky Competition in Moscow in 1970.

Although we live in an age of technology, specialisation and professionalism, the spirit of amateurism is, fortunately, still very much alive in our community. So is the desire to be individually and corporately active: a desire met by the constantly growing numbers of school orchestras which flourish despite difficulties arising from an overriding problem, the problem of school exams and the inordinate time they take up. Apart from school orchestras, there are many county and city orchestras regularly enrolling players and melodising away. In this field the pioneer was the National Youth Orchestra of Great Britain. This was founded in 1948 by the dynamic Ruth Railton whose worthy successor, Ivey Dickson, spends many weeks every year travelling from Land's End to just about everywhere, looking for—and finding—exceptionally gifted players in schools. Rehearsals, held three times every year, suffice to mould these recruits into an orchestra which attains an unbelievably high level of ensemble and artistry. Most eminent conductors agree that the National Youth Orchestra has no peer anywhere in the world. Youth and Music maintains close connections with the N.Y.O., although it facilitates also appearances of other first-class British youth orchestras, like the Kent and Essex orchestras, here and abroad.

In making out my case and proving to you how amazing our musical expansion has been, I must not overlook our music colleges, which are making strenuous efforts to modernise both their buildings and their policies. In the

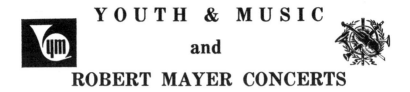

YOUTH & MUSIC

and

ROBERT MAYER CONCERTS

present

CELEBRATION CONCERT FOR YOUNG PEOPLE

A FANFARE FOR EUROPE

ROYAL FESTIVAL HALL

Saturday, 13th January 1973

LONDON SYMPHONY ORCHESTRA

Conductor
COLIN DAVIS

days of my youth British composers and performers considered it natural to finish their studies abroad, chiefly in Germany. To-day's picture is quite different. In the first place, Hitlerism destroyed the very roots of German musical life: the music teachers. Secondly, London has become the world's musical capital. Young musicians from many countries flock to our colleges to study there and to have the chance of participating in the city's musical life. While functioning as powerful magnets to young musicians at home and abroad, our music colleges are not the *sole* magnets. I need only cite two international competitions—the one for pianists held in Leeds and the Carl Flesch competition for violin and viola held in London. Some, including myself, wish that these international competitions had never been invented. The divine art of music was never intended for competition—such an activity is all too often marked by nationalism and other undesirable motives. However, they exist. Nobody can ignore them. And Britain must therefore play her part in them.

Altogether the Europe now in the making will in time obviously bring about far closer co-operation than existed in the past between Britain and the other member countries of the Common Market. It is about a hundred years ago since these other members first entered the industrial sphere in which Britain had until then been the paramount power. In music the reverse process is applying. Until fairly recent times, other countries—chiefly the Germanic countries—dominated the field of music, in which we are only now emerging as potential leaders.

In 1968 twenty six leading educationalists in the United Kingdom were invited to contribute to the *Blueprint for Education* in the next decade. It was published under the title *LOOKING FORWARD TO THE SEVENTIES.*

Among those who contributed were Lord Butler of Saffron Walden, Lord Robbins of Clare Market, Lord James of Rusholme, Sir John Newsom, Mr. Anthony Chenevix-Trench, Professor David Donnison, Archbishop Dr. Beck, Mr. Kenneth Adams and Sir Herbert Read. Sir Rober Mayer was invited to contribute his suggestions for musical education. He called them *Reflections and Projections on Music and Youth.*

REFLECTIONS AND PROJECTIONS ON MUSIC AND YOUTH

Seventy years ago

As a beginning, I feel I should declare my interests. Contrary to most contributors to this symposium, I am neither a professional musician, nor an educationist, but merely one of a dying species; a patron of music who has given his life to what may be considered constructive pioneer work. During nearly half a century I have gained practical experience in both the educational and musical fields. As a result I am firmly convinced that the English are at least as musical as other nations, that in fact, they have the potential for becoming the leaders in the world of music. This may seem to some readers an extravagant statement; I am encouraged to make it because of the remarkable changes which I have witnessed since I first came to England in 1896, changes probably set in motion through the efforts of the late Sir Henry Wood in his institution of the Promenade Concerts. It was he who first acquainted a popular audience with the world's musical literature, and the result of this tradition can be seen today in the magnificent

Reprinted from *Looking Forward to the Seventies*. Editor Peter Bander. © 1968 Colin Smythe Limited.

work done by the B.B.C. under the guidance of William Glock.

This is not all. In the period I speak of orchestral playing was at a very low level. There were different orchestras, it is true, but they were largely composed of the same players, and the deputy system, by which any player could send a deputy to an already rehearsed concert if he should have found a more lucrative engagement, could not ensure a first class performance to say the least of it. The operatic world too left even more to be desired: a short star season at Covent Garden, and an occasional visit from the two travelling companies, was all that London enjoyed. And the provinces were even worse off. The only field in which the British could then be said to compete with the European standards was that of oratorio, but even there the repertoire was limited to the old tried favourites, and a composer such as Edward Elgar was indebted to Germany for the first performances of some of his major works.

After the First World War

It was because of this state of affairs that in 1923 my wife and I were convinced that some way must be found to help those few people who were trying to create both a better musical climate and new audiences. To do this, education must be called to music's aid and we instituted the orchestral concerts for school children which bear my name. We were perhaps not alone in our wish to raise the standard, but we were probably more fundamental in our approach, and we were fortunate to have the enthusiastic support of educationists of all kinds, from teachers in primary schools to His Majesty's Inspectors, of whom three singularly gifted men were outstanding, Cyril Winn and Geoffrey Shaw, succeeded by Bernard Shore.

But the going to concerts and the joy of listening to music was not enough; it had to be continued in the making of music by the young who are always more interested in what they can do themselves than in what can be done for them. After persistent effort some authorities consented to supply instruments to those schools who would introduce orchestral playing to their pupils; and from a small beginning has grown the whole complex of music making in the form of youth orchestras—national, county, municipal and school—which is the envy of other European nations.

During the course of this article other factors will emerge which can rightly fill us with pride and optimism; however, the purpose of my observations is not to indulge in complacency, but to tell the truth and to propose what could and should be done if in the seventies we are to reach full musical development.

Education

How? there is no short cut; the best and surest method at hand is obviously education. In using that word I do not mean work done in the formal school curriculum, but rather the formation of the tastes and habits of young people outside the curriculum, and often outside the school itself. Such education in essence draws out all that is latent in an individual. It will be generally conceded that musical education can be justified on the same basic grounds as any other kind of non-vocational education. It is just as natural to teach children good music as, say, good literature. They may not understand it all. That is irrelevant. They do not fully understand all they read. The main aim is that they must be made aware of music's existence and be given the chance to make the choice for themselves, if only to counteract the pressure of less valuable counterattractions in the world in which they will emerge.

Primary schools

It is true that a certain amount of music has always been a part of primary schools' activity; but formerly it was mostly confined to the singing of hymns or to inferior music written for school use which could only be replaced gradually by works written by George Dyson, Armstrong Gibbs and others who realized that there was a field where they could operate for their own and the children's benefit. Simultaneously the non-competitive movement brought some incentive to both teachers and children. But primary schools were still deprived of good teachers, decent pianos and other requirements and broadly the child left primary school without even the ability to read music at sight. A revolution has occurred in primary schools in the last ten years, thanks to Maxwell Davies, George Self and other pioneers as well as the B.B.C. whose contribution is described later in this article. Also, children's concerts in and out of school, as well as the activities of enlightened teachers, and music advisers, resulting in school orchestras, have created a new climate.

Secondary schools

Common sense demands that these achievements should be followed up in the secondary school; unfortunately this is not the case. The impetus generated in primary schools is kept up only in respect to orchestral playing. No statistics are available about the large numbers of good orchestras which have been organized since the war. The London School Symphony Orchestra, the Leicestershire School Orchestra—the result of Mr. Stewart Mason's vision—and a few others, pay regular visits abroad where they are much acclaimed. But probably even in the seventies we will not reach the ideal whereby every secondary school possesses its own orchestra; and apart from this happy development, musical secondary education is falling far behind education in primary schools. The G.C.E. is, it seems, the enemy of music and so is paternalism, as I can illustrate by one concrete example. Recently I established direct contact with a few senior boys from a school. They got together a large group of boys who had previously not been interested in music, and have now secured for themselves the benefits deriving from my movement, Youth and Music. Thereupon I asked the headmasters of thirty-eight other schools of a similar type to give me the same chance with their pupils. Not one of them replied. Result: the pupils, without their knowledge, were deprived of the benefits which thousands of others enjoy, and of the chance of organizing matters internally, without troubling their teachers.

The plea that the money and care spent on junior pupils has been wasted unless education of the seniors is continued falls on deaf ears; it is often met by the assertion that the musical do play, and that the others are not musical and therefore, do not count. This specious argument is often an excuse for apathy and aversion to action and in any case it overlooks the fact that the large majority of people who are not sufficiently gifted to make music should be given the chance, through education, to become music-lovers.

Leisure

This point should appeal especially to those who want to prepare for the seventies when the problem of more leisure hours will be facing us. Music is probably one of the best and easiest methods at hand which can fill these hours, especially for the young who can find in it an outlet for their emotions. Modern life without music is, or should be considered un-thinkable; and secondary education should be organized accordingly.

Opera

The task of widening and improving musical education will be greatly helped by the advent of a new factor: opera. Practical experience in school and college has proved that young people are greatly drawn to opera. This is the era of visual attraction and this discovery should therefore not be surprising; more-over, it furnishes proof that, given the opportunity, the English are opera minded. The absence of opera in Britain, due to the effects of puritanism and subsequently industrialism has left a wide gap in our musical life which has only now begun to be filled by our two permanent opera houses of which we can be rightly proud. Lilian Baylis's dream has come more than true at Sadlers Wells; and thanks to Sir David Webster, George Solti and others, Covent Garden ranks among the world's leading opera houses. Whether it be the schools who perform opera on their own ground, or the large majority who do not do so, all should be given the opportunity of hearing operas in which the greatest composers have found outlet for their genius. Opera is confined at present mainly to London, though travelling companies and budding art centres reach out to other parts of the country. Youth and Music aims at letting youth benefit from and at the same time help in this expansion. Central and other authorities supporting operatic performances obviously also require public support and especially new audiences which can be made up most easily and effectively by our youth. Fifty years ago concerts given outside schools were a novelty. This is no longer the case, although for lack of concert halls and finance most concerts are still given in school; but concerts outside are naturally more exciting and stimulating, and it is hoped that educators will give a further lead by encouraging attendance in opera houses. In doing so they will have the satisfaction of also supporting the growth of opera in Britain. In the twenties Sir Thomas Beecham launched an operatic campaign, but, though a genius, used the wrong methods. People cannot be bludgeoned into going to opera. Leadership must coincide with public demand. Let youth be articulate. The need for more opera cannot be overstressed, for the growth of opera will bring to the fore much musical and artistic talent which is only latent at present.

Specially gifted children

This is not the only waste of talent. We also deprive children who are exceptionally endowed as instrumentalists of the chance to develop their gifts early enough. Heads of our conservatoires and others have stated repeatedly that such children should receive special instruction in which conventional education need not be disregarded. Menuhin and the Central

University of Houston
Music Library
106 Fine Arts
Houston, Texas 77004

Tutorial School have begun to tackle the problem of the specially talented children, but action is required on a far larger scale if we wish to advance the cause of music, not only quantitatively but also qualitatively. Where none can excel, nothing excellent can result, be the musician professional or amateur. In fact, the two are closely linked.

Teachers

The production of the right kind of teachers is obviously of paramount importance and deserves more profound discussion than is possible within the framework of this short article. The dismal conditions prevailing in the twenties have been replaced by more enlightened methods of training in music colleges, colleges of education and universities. Professor Mellers at the University of York, Professor Dart at the University of London and others hold original ideas and pursue progressive policies. The Gulbenkian Report exposed the difficulties under which our music colleges are operating owing to quite insufficient support by the Treasury. The position in the much newer colleges of education appears to have engendered less interest. It may not be unfair to say that, of course with exceptions, people often enter the music teaching profession who may be adequate musicians, but inadequate teachers, or vice versa; and there are also those lacking the experience in handling young people who, especially when adolescent, should add music proper to their interest in commercially advertised pop music. For the task of teaching in primary and secondary schools we require far more teachers who possess, and who can stimulate creative imagination; who spurn uniformity; who use the examination system to a minimum extent; who do not command, but who attempt to inspire their pupils; and above all, who educate through enjoyment, the love and joy of making and listening to music. Foreigners are amazed at the independent authority which our central and local governments delegate to headmasters who, in turn, pass it on to heads of departments. Long may this continue, provided that in the seventies qualified teachers will definitely secure for music especially in secondary schools, its proper status.

Radio and television

Fortunately influences coming from outside school have already helped to raise the status of music and to improve the musical climate in schools. Foremost have been broadcasting and Youth and Music. For understandable reasons I will not elaborate on the latter. As to the former, I must go back to 1924 when the late Mary Somerville heard, when she was by chance in a village schoolroom, a broadcast talk on music by Walford Davies. The talk was not intended for a classroom audience, but hearing it in this situation made Miss Somerville see the potential value of broadcasting in school education. At first there was some opposition from the teaching profession who saw the use of radio in the classroom as unfair competition, but in 1929 the Central Council for School Broadcasting was founded, and ever since the B.B.C. has worked hand in hand with the teaching profession.

Music has always been at the heart of school broadcasts—for instance, about 12,000 schools take the series 'Singing Together'. Broadcasts have been particularly valuable in schools where there are no teachers confident enough to take music unaided. But because broadcasts are planned to keep abreast of the latest developments in music teaching, and can tap unrivalled musical resources, even gifted music teachers may find them stimulating to use. The emphasis nowadays is on active and creative participation by the classroom audience, with children playing many of the instruments that were popularized by Carl Orff. In 1963 television joined radio in presenting a regular series of programmes to both primary and secondary schools; and in the hands of John Hosier, who moved over from radio to start the new programmes, there has been an emphasis on commissioning new works from leading composers to start a repertoire for primary schools of good music that children can perform, both vocally and instrumentally, entirely on their own. At a time when Britain denigrates its achievements, it is pleasant to know that B.B.C. television is unique in the world in presenting a regular and committed series of music programmes to schools.

Resident Quartets

There are other new ideas, conceived outside school, which can help education. One is the scheme to attach resident quartets to universities and towns. So far the scheme has been ratified in Edinburgh, Dartington, Keele and Harlow: a tiny beginning compared with over two hundred resident quartets in American colleges. This innovation can be of real constructive value if the ensemble performs not only for a college or other body, but for the community at large, academic or not; and if, in addition, the players also teach, and lead nonprofessional orchestras in and outside school or college. The scarcity of public concert halls has already resulted in the use of school halls for public concerts, for the enjoyment of the community. Members of the resident quartet, by participating in the lives of school and community, can help remove barriers between them and thereby engender a much needed common interest and civic pride.

Patronage

In the early twenties when the (then) London County Council refused to support concerts and opera in London, the Government gave a grant of £25,000 to Covent Garden which was abandoned owing to the pettiness of other musical interests. The present policy adopted by the Government has opened a new chapter in our musical history, and, largely thanks to the leadership of Miss Jennie Lee and Lord Goodman, the grants made through the Arts Council are constantly rising. Local authorities, especially the Greater London Council, are also extending their patronage, and so are Foundations—Gulbenkian, Peter Stuyvesant, Leverhulme, Munster,

Vaughan Williams and others. Unfortunately industry as a whole has not yet realized the role which it should play in participating in the country's musical development; social reasons alone point to the wisdom of action in the seventies. When considering the future the I.L.E.A. would be well advised to change its policy of providing outside operatic or concert performances free to young people because they are given in school. This ruling is based on a hundred-year-old law made when social conditions were entirely different. Young people today have the money to pay for what they want, and they will value far more an event which they have chosen and paid for. Further, if they are simply sent to a concert or an opera by the school, the majority will simply relate this in their mind with lessons, from which they will be relieved when they go out into the world. The exact opposite is desirable—they should regard the arts as something which will add to enjoyment in their entire life.

Barbican Scheme

The city authorities have also evinced a new attitude to the arts by sanctioning the Barbican Scheme whereby the Guildhall of Music and the new Concert Hall will be built next to each other, with the London Symphony Orchestra serving as resident orchestra. Its members will also teach in the school. Performing and instructing will thus be in the new pattern, as in the case of resident quartets. I cannot refrain here from comment on the dual value of this scheme: it can be a focal point for the members of Youth and Music who work in the City of London; and they in turn can help to provide the audiences necessary for the scheme's success.

Conclusions

To conclude. I have endeavoured to present some facets of a very complex situation, and to depict the real progress which has been made in various directions and which justified the optimism expressed at the beginning of this article. The task confronting us in the years ahead requires above all a new spirit; a burning faith in music and the creation of a point of vantage overlooking the entire position. At present we are still bedevilled by a separatism shown in the barriers which exist between the various types of schools and colleges and also between both of them and the rest of society. People may be doing excellent work in their special spheres; but this is by definition very limited. Education and music are divided traditionally by a gap which must be filled by co-ordination, so that each component part knows and profits from what the others are doing. The present situation is not unlike an old-fashioned office, composed of numerous little rooms, each being used by separate interests. Let us scrap it and replace it by one spacious floor, light, free of partitions, the requisite for enthusiastic collaboration. Consolidation is the watch-word in business and could well be copied in the field of music, provided it can be organized within the framework of individualism and enterprise, a pre-requisite of an era of unprecedented revolutionary changes in society. Democracies are generally suspicious of anyone functioning outside the common herd of mankind and therefore lean heavily on conformity; let us beware of this enemy of the arts.

The musical development in Britain and U.S.A. during the last forty years has been phenomenal, yet we have in Britain large regions which are underdeveloped, or even undeveloped. Reformers therefore have a tremendous task ahead of them before they can claim that we are a musical nation, meaning that the ordinary man feels that music is part of his life. As I have endeavoured to show in this article, this goal can be reached most quickly and effectively by inspiring the youth of the country.

MY credo remains the same as it has always been: a burning faith in music and in Britain's innate musicality. If I have contributed constructively towards that end, I feel that I have not lived in vain.

"*Which individual has done most to foster music in this country during the past half century? Names like Beecham and Wood immediately spring to mind. But I suspect that history may nominate Robert Mayer.*"

Peter Heyworth in the OBSERVER

BIOGRAPHICAL DATA

MAYER, Sir ROBERT, C.H. (1973); Kt. (1938); born 5 June 1879, Mannheim, Germany, third son of Emil and Lucie Mayer née Seligman; educated at the Mannheim Konservatorium.

LL.D.(h.c.) Leeds; Mus.D.(h.c.) Cleveland, Ohio, U.S.A.; D.Sc.(h.c.) City of London.

Hon. Fellow: Royal Academy of Music, Royal College of Music, Guildhall School of Music, Trinity College of Music.

Grand Cross of Merit, Federal Republic of Germany; Ordre de la Couronne, Belgium.

Founder: *Robert Mayer Concerts for Children* (1923) jointly with Dorothy Moulton-Mayer, Mus.D.(h.c.) T.C.D.; Co-Founder with Sir Thomas Beecham: *London Philharmonic Orchestra* (1932); *Elizabeth Fry Foundation*. American Representative *'Save the Children Fund'* (1940-1943); Hon. Treasurer *'World University Service'* (1946-1955); Trustee *'Dorothy Moulton-Mayer Foundation for Music'*, Republic of Ireland (1952); Founder: *Youth & Music* (1954); formerly Co-Chairman *London Symphony Orchestra;* President (until 1973), now Hon. President *'World Jeunesses Musicales Orchestra';* Vice President *Royal College of Music;* President *London Schools Symphony Orchestra;* President

Saffron Walden Music Club; Founder *'New Musical Harlow';* Founder *Transatlantic Foundation Anglo-American Scholarships.* Member of Council: *National Music Council; English Chamber Orchestra; Wind Music Society; Anglo-Israel Society; Live Music; International Music Seminar.* Patron: *EEC Orchestra; International Festival of Youth Orchestras.*

Publications: *Young People in Trouble; Crescendo; Robert Mayer Concerts for Children* (Series); *My First Hundred Years; Reflections and Projections on Music and Youth; Anatomy of a Miracle.*

INDEX